TWO BROTHERS, FOUR HANDS

The Artists
ALBERTO AND DIEGO GIACOMETTI

Jan Greenberg and Sandra Jordan

Illustrated by Hadley Hooper

NEAL PORTER BOOKS

HOLIDAY HOUSE / NEW YORK

The genius is in the details.
To Jennifer Browne with gratitude —J.G. and S.J.

For Hugh —H.H.

1901–1918
IN THE SWISS VILLAGE OF STAMPA,
surrounded by mountains so high
that in winter their shadows fill the valley,
live two brothers.

Alberto and Diego Giacometti,
born only a year apart,
are as different as brothers can be.

Their father, a painter, gives his children pencils
and paper to sketch the beauty around them.
Everyone agrees that Alberto
is the genius of the family. The artist.
Rough-and-tumble games don't appeal to Alberto.
He is content to read all day
or sit in his father's studio, drawing.
He loves the smell of paint and turpentine.

Diego doesn't care for school or books.

He roams the countryside, spying on foxes, otters, and deer.

Fearless, he scales steep ridges and skis all the way down.

One a daredevil, the other a dreamer, they are tied to each other

as if by some secret understanding.

Diego looks up to his big brother

and often does his chores, so that Alberto can keep reading.

5

At age thirteen Alberto makes his first sculpture.
Diego is his model.
With a compass, Alberto measures his brother's face,
the space between the bottom of the nose and lips,
the size of the eyes and the space between the eyes.
The head grows beneath his fingers.

On his first Christmas holiday from boarding school
Alberto sets off alone to travel to his village.
During the long wait for a train, he spies a book
about the great French sculptor Rodin.
Very expensive!
But he has to have it.

AUGUSTE
RODIN

Late that night the train reaches his stop. The sleigh that will carry him over
the mountain pass to Stampa doesn't leave until morning.
With no money left and nowhere to sleep, what can he do but walk?

A narrow road, five thousand feet high in the Alps,
pitch-black and icy.
Alberto, half frozen, slips and slides all the way home,
still clutching his precious book.

1919–1921

Alberto has no desire to go to college.

He wants to travel, to learn about art.

Along the way he takes classes in artists' studios.

In Italy he haunts museums and churches.

He fills whole journals with sketches and notes to himself.

1922–1933

Finally he feels ready to study in Paris,

the center of the art world.

There, young artists, poets, and playwrights gather in bars and cafés.

They are impressed

by Alberto's spellbinding conversation.

He is impressed

by the way they turn their dreams and fantasies into art.

The group call themselves Surrealists.

Art should come from the imagination, they say, not from life.

Alberto adapts their ideas into his sculpture.

Galleries in Paris take notice and display his work.

Diego bounces from one tight spot to another.
Petty thievery. Smuggling!
His mother, fed up with her handsome but shiftless son,
tells him to go to Paris.
His brother can use an extra pair of hands.
That Alberto needs him is all it takes.

Diego moves to Paris.

Alberto finds a studio on Rue Hippolyte-Maindron.

He and Diego pile their few possessions into a wheelbarrow and roll it through the streets to a tumbledown building.

A beaten-earth floor.
A cold-water tap and a toilet down the hall.
No kitchen, not even a hot plate.
Skylights that leak rain and snow.

A small studio,
but enough room
to make art.

Alberto, protective of his brother,
encourages him to take art lessons.
Diego lasts a week.
Alberto puts out brushes and canvases.
Diego tries to paint but gives up.

His brother worries.
His mother worries.
Diego shrugs.

1934–1939

Meanwhile, despite praise in the press
and, *yes*, a few sales,
Alberto grows dissatisfied.
Surrealists insist on art rules he can no longer follow,
rules that clash with what he feels in his heart.

He decides to go back to sculpting from a live model.

Art dealers quickly drop him.

Friends cross the street if they see him coming.

Still, Alberto has made up his mind.

He will sit on a stool in his studio

and try to re-create what he sees.

Alberto doesn't see the way others see.

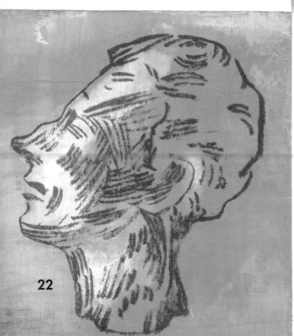

Alberto says, "A single human face can give an artist
the subject matter to fill a lifetime."
Every day for five years
patient Diego poses in the same position,
for the same bust Alberto stubbornly builds of plaster,
trims back to minuscule size, or destroys.

Again and again
Alberto tries to capture in plaster and in paint
the mystery of what makes Diego's head Diego.

Working around the studio,
Diego finds he is good with his hands.

But Alberto, the once-confident boy
who thought he could draw anything,
now doubts himself.

He starts with a sculpture
the size of his forearm,
then cuts and scrapes
until the work is tinier
than his thumb.

Late at night over dinners with friends, he talks and talks about his struggles.

25

Summer 1940. World War II.
Invading German troops march toward Paris.
Terrified, people flee the city.
The brothers take the crowded road south,
hoping to catch a boat for America.
Alberto rides a borrowed bike.
Diego and his girlfriend, Nelly,
pedal a bicycle built for two.

They pass through burning towns,
the air leaden with metal-gray smoke.
Planes drone overhead.
The rattle of artillery erupts like thunder,
shooting fiery sparks across the dark sky.
They hide in a ditch, bullets flying all around them.
After five frightening days they retreat to Paris.

27

1942–1945

While Diego remains in Paris to guard their studio,

Alberto leaves for Switzerland to join their mother.

He rents a dreary room more decrepit than his studio in Paris.

Even he doesn't understand why he continues

to carve his plaster figures smaller and smaller.

Diego begs, "Make sculpture of a less ridiculous size."

His adoring mother scolds, "Your father never did that."

28

Alberto wrestles with his art,
but life is not totally bleak.
He falls in love with a young woman named Annette.
One day she will be his wife.

Alberto fears for Diego in Paris,
where German soldiers prowl the streets.
People are arrested for no reason.
Food is scarce.
How will he live?
Diego is resourceful.
He patches together odd jobs.

Fonderie

To please Alberto,
he becomes expert at
casting objects in bronze
from plaster molds,
polishing the bronze,
and brushing the
surfaces with acid
to produce patinas of
green, gold, or black.

May 8, 1945

Germany surrenders.

Parisians celebrate in the streets.

Diego adopts a tame fox from a returning
prisoner of war.

In spite of her musky odor,
he names her Miss Rose and teaches her tricks.

Four months later, on an ordinary fall day,
Alberto reappears in Paris
with all his figurines packed in six large matchboxes.
He finds the once-dapper Diego
dressed in shabby clothes,
his slick black hair now gray and unruly.
The war was hard, but Diego saved his brother's studio.
Not even the brushes had been moved.

But what is the stench in Diego's workshop?
"Miss Rose survived the horrors of war," Diego says,
"so I'm not bothered by the smell."

Alberto, who does not share his brother's affection for the fox,
leaves the door to the street open.
Miss Rose disappears into the night forever.

Happy to have his brother back,
Diego bites his tongue.
Yet years later he makes a candelabra for Alberto's birthday.
At the base, a little bronze fox head peeks out.

July 6, 1946

Annette arrives in Paris to live with Alberto.
In a plain room across the hall from his studio,
he sets pretty red clay tiles on the dirt floor
and paints a still life of flowers on the wall to welcome her.

The brothers are poor, with no money for coal in winter
or a secondhand coat for Annette, shivering in the razor-sharp wind.
To keep going, they borrow from friends, live on bread and cheese,
often without the cheese.

1947

Now that Alberto has settled into his old studio,
he no longer needs to whittle down his sculptures.
Instead he makes tall, slender, mysterious figures,
held to the earth only by the weight of their feet.

He makes heads with shoulders so craggy they might have been hacked from the mountains of the brothers' childhood.

The war ended with much of Europe in chaos—bombed-out cities, the homeless and displaced wandering everywhere.

Alberto's skeletal, lonely figures are survivors. They rise up courageously from these ruins of war.

People are moved by the truth in Alberto's sculptures.
They express a new spirit in art.

"You must go on. I can't go on. I'll go on," says
Alberto's friend, the playwright Samuel Beckett.

An art dealer from New York City
visits the studio.
He wants to exhibit Alberto's work.
A major one-man show.
A big splash.
Finally Alberto's chance has come.

There is much to do.
Sculptures.
Drawings.
Paintings
and more sculptures.
Kneading, gouging, pressing, caressing,
carving, smoothing,
in quick strokes his fingers etch marks on
the plaster's rough surface.

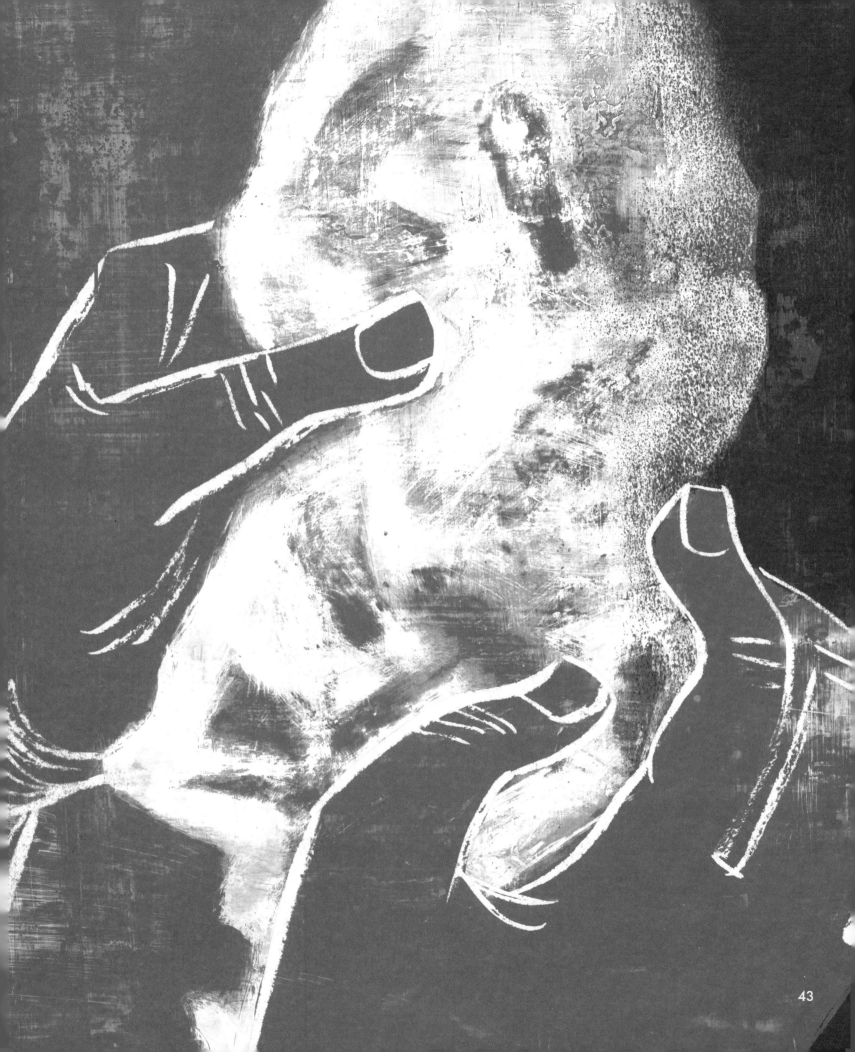

On some early mornings Diego finds Alberto
standing in front of a plaster head, staring at it,
tired, yet not able to stop.
"Go to bed,"
Diego tells his big brother.
"Go to bed."

Diego fashions thin constructions of wire
to support the willowy figures.

He builds bases to balance them
on their outsized feet.

He makes molds of the finished
pieces and delivers them to
the foundry to be cast
in bronze.

He slaves over patinas until
his picky brother nods approval.
His hand touches every sculpture.

45

January–February 1948
In New York, Alberto's artworks are a hit.
Everybody is talking, writing, and
looking, looking, looking.

With success come fame and money.
Alberto gives away careless handfuls of cash
to his models, to friends, and, of course, to Diego.
The rest he stashes in a shoebox under the bed.
He refuses to move because,
he insists,
"Artists should live in humble surroundings."

Diego has a studio next to Alberto's.
There he works on his own projects,
sculptures of animals he stalked as a child—
watchful owls, frogs, a shy doe,
and the occasional snake.
He uses these creatures to decorate handcrafted
furniture for the few people who know about it.

The more requests for
Alberto's sculptures pour in,
the less time Diego has for
his own designs.

Alberto says, "Diego has talent to burn,"
but that doesn't stop him
from counting on his brother's time and attention.
Diego doesn't mind.
Alberto's art always comes first.

1965–1966
The years pass.
Alberto receives many honors.
The great Museum of Modern Art offers him a show.
Even though Alberto is in poor health,
he travels to New York for the opening.

FRESH
BREAD

TEL

PARK

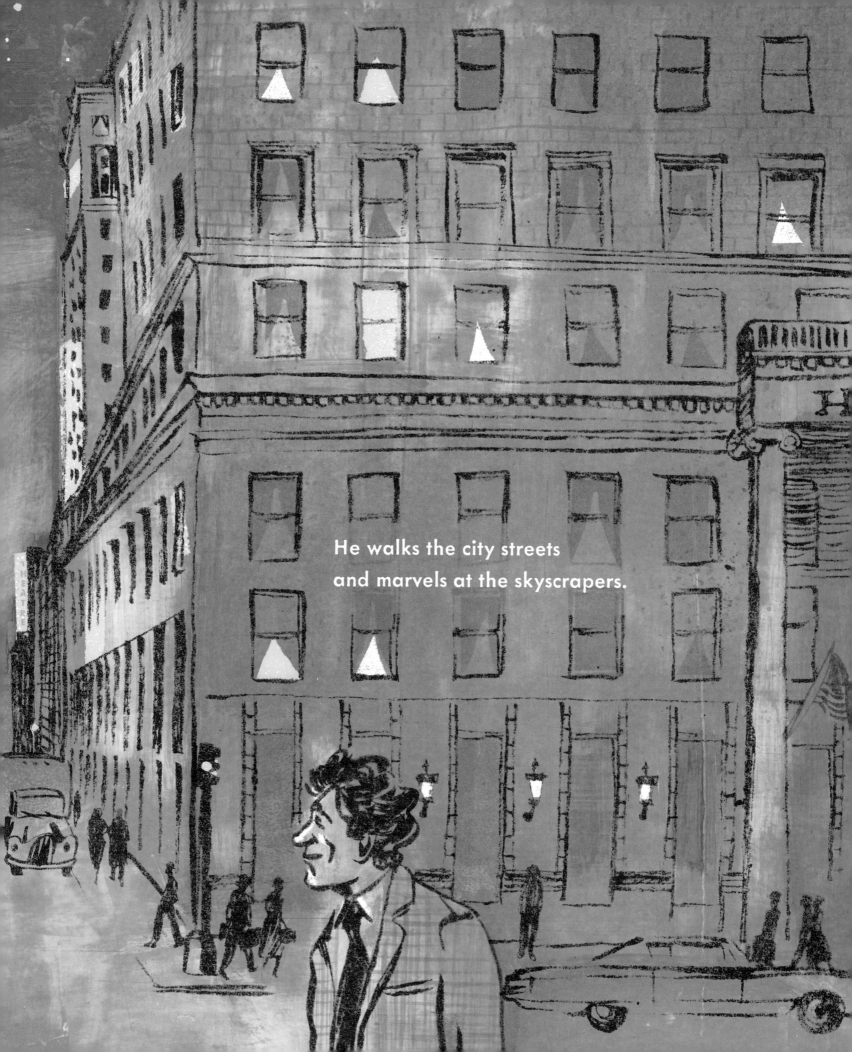

He walks the city streets
and marvels at the skyscrapers.

He returns to Paris, feeling weak.
Annette and Diego persuade him to go to a hospital
in Switzerland, not far from where the brothers were born.
Days later Alberto dies.

Diego, alone, cries to their friends,
"What is there for me to do now?"

As if his hands decide for him,
he starts making more objects,
furniture so magical that one sees sculpture
and forgets its function.

A horse nips at a tree leaf.
Frogs perch on a tabletop.
Cats stare at birds
through table legs.

When he bothers to sign his work,
he refuses to profit from the famous Giacometti name
and writes simply "Diego" or "DG."
"My brother was the artist," he says.
"I am merely a craftsman."

Diego carves Alberto's headstone himself.
On the grave he attaches his brother's last work,
a plaster figure cast in bronze.
One of Diego's sculptures, a little pigeon, stands nearby.

Two brothers, four hands.

Looking at
Alberto Giacometti's *Walking Man*

A sculpture exists in three dimensions. It exists in space, and you can view it from all sides. But how do we talk about it?

First describe what you see. Is the sculpture a figure, an object, or an abstract form? An abstract form means the artwork has no recognizable subject matter. In a book, museum, or gallery, take a look at the label. It will tell you the title, size, material, and the year the sculpture was made.

The 6½-foot-tall man is walking with hands by his sides, his body thrust forward. The hands and feet look large, out of proportion. He seems to be walking on a muddy base that sticks to his back heel and toe.

Using the elements of art—color, shape, line, and texture—let's describe some sensory properties of the artwork, those we perceive through our senses of touch, sight, hearing, taste, and smell.

lines—straight and angular. The figure looks masculine, but cannot be identified as a recognizable person.

form/shape—elongated and stiff. The man is tall, and so thin that you can see on his chest the outlines of his ribs.

texture—lumpy, uneven, as if the artist left his finger marks everywhere

color (or patina on the bronze metal)—gray with touches of brown

Alberto Giacometti
Walking Man II, 1960
Bronze, 74 3/16 x 11 x 43 9/16 in.
National Gallery of Art, Washington
Gift of Enid A. Haupt
Art © 2018 Alberto Giacometti Estate/
VAGA at ARS, NY / ADAGP, Paris

If he could speak, what might he say? Would he speak in a whisper or in a loud, booming voice?

If the figure suddenly came to life, how would he walk? Slow or fast? What qualities of the sculpture give us a hint?

The last and most important question is: What is the feeling expressed? Is he sad or happy? What is the expression on his face? Although he is anchored to the ground by his large, heavy feet, his thin, bony body gives him a feeling of fragility. But at the same time, by his forward stride, we know he isn't indecisive or unsure. We don't know where he came from or where he is going, but there is a sense that he is single-minded about getting there.

The Giacometti Family in Stampa, about 1910. Left to right, top: Alberto, Bruno, Giovanni, Annetta; bottom: Diego and Ottilia

TIMELINE

1868 Giovanni Giacometti, father of the brothers Alberto and Diego, is born. He becomes an important Swiss painter.

1900 Giovanni marries Annetta Stampa, a handsome and strong-minded woman with her own small fortune.

1901 October 10 Alberto is born in Borgonovo, Switzerland, to Annetta and Giovanni.

1902 November 16 Diego is born in Borgonovo.

1903 Sister Ottilia is born. A weaver, she dies in her twenties, leaving behind one son.

1906 The family moves to a farmhouse in the town of Stampa. There is no electricity until 1922 and no running water until 1927, but they do have one of two gas lamps in the village. Giovanni's art studio is next door in an old converted barn. Alberto later says, "I can't imagine any happier childhood than the one I spent with my father and my whole family." (Hohl, p.13)

1907 Brother Bruno is born. He will become an important Swiss architect and live to be 105.

1914 August 14 World War I begins. Most of Europe is fighting, but Switzerland, where the Giacometti family lives, stays neutral.

1915 Alberto goes to a boarding school called Schiers near Chur, Switzerland. His artistic ability makes him popular. He is given his own studio, and boys line up down the hall to have their portraits drawn.

1917 Diego joins Alberto at Schiers.
April The U.S. enters World War I.

1918 November Armistice is signed in Europe. The war ends.

1919 Alberto takes a leave of absence from his school and never returns. He doesn't graduate. Diego happily leaves at the same time.

1919–1921 Alberto attends art school in Geneva.

Giovanni Giacometti
The Lamp, 1912
Oil on canvas, 55 1/8 x 51 in.
The Museum of Art, Zurich, Switzerland

1921 Alberto visits museums in Italy, where he sees an ancient Egyptian head and battle chariot that have a big impact on his ideas about art. He stays with his cousins in Rome.

1922 January 1 Alberto moves to Paris. He attends classes at the Académie de la Grande Chaumière for five years, while slowly establishing himself as a sculptor.

1924 Diego leaves home, but visits his mother in Stampa for a month every year until she dies.

1925 After working at various short-term jobs and traveling, Diego comes to Paris to be with his brother.

1929 Alberto is invited by André Breton, the leader of the Surrealists, to officially join the group. Alberto sells some of his Surrealist pieces.

October 29 The U.S. stock market crashes, triggering a worldwide financial depression.

1929–1940 To earn money, Alberto and Diego start making decorative objects for designer Jean-Michel Frank. They also make jewelry for fashion designer Elsa Schiaparelli.

1933 Alberto and Diego's father, Giovanni Giacometti, dies.

1934 Alberto begins to pull away from the Surrealist group.

1935 February The Surrealists formally expel Alberto from the group. He becomes friends with artist Pablo Picasso.

1936 The director of the Museum of Modern Art in New York City includes five pieces of Alberto's work in a show called *Cubism and Abstract Art*. He buys *The Palace at 4 a.m.* for the MoMA collection.

1937 Alberto and playwright Samuel Beckett meet and become friends.

1939 September 1 Germany invades Poland.

September 3 Britain and France declare war on Germany. Switzerland stays neutral, so Alberto and Diego cannot be drafted.

Photograph by Alexander Liberman
Alberto Giacometti, his brother Diego, and wife, Annette, in Paris studio, circa 1954
Alexander Liberman Collection of Photographs
Getty Research Institute, Los Angeles, (2000.R.19)
© J. Paul Getty Trust
Art © 2018 Alberto Giacometti Estate / VAGA at ARS, NY / ADAGP, Paris

1941 The German army marches toward Paris.

December 7 Japan bombs Pearl Harbor, Hawaii. The U.S. enters World War II.

December 31 Alberto moves to Switzerland to live with his mother and his sister Ottilia's son.

1942–1943 During the war, Diego makes his first animal sculptures. He earns money by designing perfume bottles and stands for display shelves. Diego's skill at making bases, stands, and supports for Alberto eventually leads into his furniture-making.

1945 September Alberto returns to Paris.

1946 July 7 Annette Arm, a woman Alberto met in Geneva, moves to Paris to be with him. She becomes one of his chief models.

1947 Alberto starts painting regularly for the first time since the 1920s.

1948 January and February Alberto has a one-man show at Pierre Matisse's gallery in New York City. French philosopher Jean-Paul Sartre writes an essay for the catalog of Alberto's work. The Tate Museum in London buys two paintings and the sculpture *Man Pointing*.

1949 Alberto and Annette marry.

1951 Alberto begins his long association with the Maeght Gallery in Paris.

1955 The first retrospectives of Alberto's work are held in museums in London and Germany.

1962 Alberto is invited to the Venice Biennale with a solo exhibition and awarded the Grand Prix for sculpture.

1964 January 25 Alberto and Diego's mother, Annetta Giacometti, dies.

1965 Alberto and Annette make a trip to New York City for the opening of a retrospective exhibition of his work at the Museum of Modern Art.

1966 January 11 Alberto dies of congestive heart failure in Chur, Switzerland.

January 15 Alberto is buried in Borgonovo next to his parents' graves. People come to the little town from all over Europe and the United States to pay their respects.

After Alberto dies, Diego renews his efforts to create furniture and sculpture that will end up making him famous. He creates furniture and fixtures for the café at the Maeght Foundation in St-Paul-de-Vence, France.

Photograph by Gordon Parks
Untitled, Paris, France, 1951
Courtesy and copyright The Gordon Parks Foundation
Art © 2018 Alberto Giacometti Estate / VAGA at ARS, NY / ADAGP, Paris

1973 Diego designs the fixtures for the Chagall Museum in Nice, France.

1985 July 15 At the age of 82, Diego collapses and dies in the hospital three days after a cataract operation. Just months later the Musée Picasso, for which he designed all the furniture and fixtures, opens in Paris.

1986 An extensive collection of Diego's work is given to the Musée des Arts Décoratifs in Paris following a retrospective exhibition.

NOTES ON THE TEXT

Page 3   In the Swiss village of Stampa: Stampa is in the Bregaglia, a dark valley running east-west between high peaks in the Swiss Alps.

Page 4   Their father, a painter: Giovanni Giacometti was an internationally recognized artist. The brothers and their siblings grew up in a house surrounded by his paintings, and sat at dinner in small walnut chairs he carved for them.

Page 7   He spies a book about the great French sculptor Rodin: Hohl, p. 18.

Page 14   Petty thievery. Smuggling!: Lord, *Biography*, pp. 89–92. James Lord (1922–2009) knew both of the Giacometti brothers intimately and often watched them work.

Page 14   His mother . . . tells him to go to Paris: Marchesseau, p. 10.

Page 17   A beaten-earth floor: Peppiatt, p. 118. Simone de Beauvoir (1908–1986), a French intellectual, feminist, and best-selling writer, described the studio in a letter she wrote to a friend.

Page 23   "A single human face": Peppiatt, p. 114.

Page 23   the same bust Alberto stubbornly builds of plaster: Plaster is a dry powder of limestone and sand mixed with water into a paste that gets very hard when it dries. In the artists' studio, Alberto used it to make sculptures. Diego used it to make molds of his brother's sculptures before casting them into bronze and other materials.

Diego Giacometti
Headwaiter Cat, Bronze,
circa 1965. Height: 11 1/2 in.
Private Collection
Art © 2018 Artists Rights Society (ARS),
New York / ADAGP, Paris

Page 25   Late at night . . . he talks and talks: Hohl, p. 115. Many of the people who knew Alberto mention his compelling conversation. Simone de Beauvoir said, "A diary is useless for this sort of thing: to keep any sort of record of the irresistible conversation between Sartre and Giacometti needs a tape recorder."

Page 26   The brothers take the crowded road: Lord, *Biography*, p. 213; Sylvester, p. 94.

Page 28   "Make sculpture of a less ridiculous size": Lord, *Biography*, p. 217.

Page 28   "Your father never did that": Lord, *Biography*, p. 223.

Page 34   six large matchboxes: Hohl, p. 108. Art-book publisher Albert Skira told about visiting Alberto as he was leaving Switzerland with his matchboxes.

Page 35   But what is the stench: Lord, *Biography*, p. 247.

Page 36   he sets pretty red clay tiles: Peppiatt, p. 8. The description of Alberto decorating the room for Annette is from Jean Genet (1910–1986), French playwright, essayist, poet, and thief.

Page 37   a secondhand coat: Hohl, p. 120. Simone de Beauvoir wrote letters about Alberto and her admiration for Alberto's young wife, who came to live with him.

Page 41   a new spirit in art: Hohl, p. 115. Françoise Gilot (1926–), an artist and writer, quoted the opinion of her then-partner, Pablo Picasso (1881–1973), one of the most influential artists of the twentieth century, on the importance of Alberto's work. Picasso and Giacometti had many long conversations.

Alberto Giacometti
The Chariot, 1950
Bronze, 64 5/8 x 27 x 26 3/8 in.
Gift of Enid A. Haupt
National Gallery of Art, Washington
Art © 2018 Alberto Giacometti Estate / VAGA at ARS, NY / ADAGP, Paris

Page 41 **"You must go on"**: These are the final lines of *The Unnamable*, the last in a trilogy of novels by Irish writer Samuel Beckett (1906–1989). He and Alberto used to take long, rambling late-night walks around Paris.

Page 42 **An art dealer from New York City**: The dealer was Pierre Matisse (1900–1989), youngest son of the famous French artist Henri Matisse. Pierre moved to New York in the 1930s and started an art gallery there.

Diego Giacometti
Armchair with lion heads, front feet with lion's claws, Bronze
circa 1970. Height: 32 in.
Private Collection
Art © 2018 Artists Rights Society (ARS), New York / ADAGP, Paris

Page 42 **Kneading, gouging**: Lord, *Biography*, p. 121.

Page 44 **"Go to bed"**: Lord, *Biography*, p. 321.

Page 45 **His hand touches every sculpture**: Robert Wernick essay in Francisci.

Page 46 **In New York, Alberto's artworks are a hit**: Hohl, p. 130. In 2015 *Man Pointing*, a sculpture he made in 1948, sold at Christie's auction house for $140 million.

Page 46 **Everybody is talking**: Hohl, p. 134. "I took my hat off to him," said American artist Barnett Newman. Writer and art critic Dore Ashton said, "Nobody has provoked more discussion than Giacometti."

Page 47 **a shoebox under the bed**: Hohl, p. 150.

Page 47 **"Artists should live in humble surroundings"**: Peppiatt, p. 142. Alberto bought his brother a house and his wife an apartment, but he refused to move from Hippolyte. The spartan conditions he continued to live in after he was rich and famous became part of his mystique.

Page 49 **"Diego has talent to burn"**: Lord, *Biography*, p. 331.

Page 53 **"What is there for me to do now?"**: Robert Wernick essay in Francisci.

Page 54 **furniture so magical**: In September 2012, one of Diego's coffee tables sold at Christie's auction house for $1,673,482.

Page 56 **On the grave he attaches Alberto's last work**: Diego made a plaster cast of his brother's last sculpture of French photographer Eli Lotar. Eight bronze copies were made later. Robert Wernick essay in Francisci.

Sadly the sculpture by Alberto and the pigeon by Diego were stolen.

Diego Giacometti
Ostrich, Bronze, and ostrich egg, circa 1977. Height: 20 in.
Private Collection
Art © 2018 Artists Rights Society (ARS), New York / ADAGP, Paris

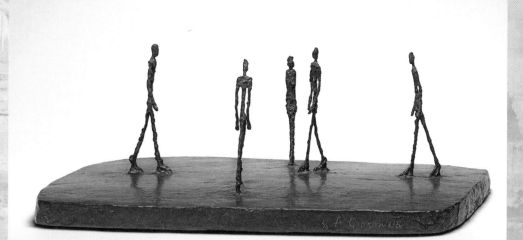

Alberto Giacometti, The City Square 1948/1949, Bronze
9 7/16 x 25 1/2 x 16 in., Gift of Enid A. Haupt, National Gallery of Art, Washington
Art © 2018 Alberto Giacometti Estate / VAGA at ARS, NY / ADAGP, Paris

Alberto Giacometti
Portrait of David Sylvester, 1960
Oil on canvas
45 ¾ x 35 in.
Photo by Robert Pettus
Private collection
Art © 2018 Alberto Giacometti Estate / VAGA at ARS, NY / ADAGP, Paris

BIBLIOGRAPHY

Baudot, Francois. *Diego Giacometti*. New York: Assouline, 2001.

Bonnefoy, Yves. *Alberto Giacometti*. New York: Assouline, 2001.

Boutonnet, Christian, and Rafael Ortiz. *Diego Giacometti*. With a preface by James Lord. Paris: Les Editions de l'Amateur & Galerie L'Arc en Seine, 2003.

Francisci, Françoise, ed. *Diego Giacometti. Catalogue de l'oeuvre*. Volume I. With additional text by Robert Wernick and Claude Delay. Paris: Editions Eolia, 1986.

Freemont, Diane. "The Visible and the Invisible in Art: The Secret Space of the Image," http://aras.org/sites/default/files/docs/00026Fremont.pdf

Genet, Jean. *The Studio of Giacometti*. London: Grey Tiger Books, 2014.

Hohl, Reinhold, ed. *Giacometti: A Biography in Pictures*. Ostfildern-Ruit: Hatje, 1998.

Lord, James. *Giacometti, A Biography*. New York: Farrar, Straus and Giroux, 1986.

Lord, James. *A Giacometti Portrait*. New York: Farrar, Straus and Giroux, 1980.

Marchesseau, Daniel. *Diego Giacometti*. New York: Harry N. Abrams, 1987.

Peppiatt, Michael. *In Giacometti's Studio*. New Haven: Yale University Press, 2010.

Sylvester, David. *Looking at Giacometti*. With photographs by Patricia Matisse. New York: Henry Holt, 1996.

Wiesinger, Véronique, ed. *Alberto Giacometti: A Retrospective*. Malaga, Spain: Museo Picasso Málaga & Poligrafa, 2012. Exhibition catalog.

ACKNOWLEDGMENTS

As always, it takes many hands to make a book. We appreciate the help of Simon Kelly, Ph.D., Curator, and head of Department of Modern and Contemporary Art at the Saint Louis Art Museum for his good and useful thoughts; Ronnie Greenberg, whose passion for Diego Giacometti's furniture was contagious; and Mike Martin, who photographed the Diego Giacometti pieces.

At Holiday House / Neal Porter Books, we'd like to thank our longtime editor Neal Porter of Neal Porter Books, our partner in many of our art travels; our designer, the calm and buoyant Jennifer Browne; Lisa Lee, Director of Production; George Newman, copy editor; and Louisa Brady, who makes sure nothing is left behind.

Neal Porter Books

Text copyright © 2019 by Jan Greenberg and Sandra Jordan

Illustrations copyright © 2019 by Hadley Hooper

All Rights Reserved

HOLIDAY HOUSE is registered in the U.S. Patent and Trademark Office.

Printed and bound in July 2018 at Toppan Leefung, DongGuan City, China.

The art for this book was created with traditional materials—paint and ink—scanned and finished in Photoshop.

Book design by Jennifer Browne

www.holidayhouse.com

First Edition

10 9 8 7 6 5 4 3 2 1

Library of Congress Cataloging-in-Publication Data

Names: Greenberg, Jan, 1942– author. | Jordan, Sandra (Sandra Jane Fairfax) | Hooper, Hadley, illustrator.

Title: Two brothers, four hands : Alberto & Diego Giacometti / Jan Greenberg & Sandra Jordan ; illustrations by Hadley Hooper.

Description: First edition. | New York : Holiday House, 2019. | "Neal Porter Books." | Includes bibliographical references. | Audience: Ages 7–10. | Audience: Grades 4 to 6.

Identifiers: LCCN 2018024184 | ISBN 9780823441709 (hardcover)

Subjects: LCSH: Giacometti, Alberto, 1901–1966—Juvenile literature. | Giacometti, Diego—Juvenile literature. | Artists—Switzerland—Biography—Juvenile literature.

Classification: LCC N6853.G49 G74 2019 | DDC 709.2--dc23 LC record available at https://lccn.loc.gov/2018024184